fragrant candles

A practical guide to making
candles for the home & garden

fragrant candles

RHONDDA CLEARY

SALLY MILNER PUBLISHING

This book is dedicated
to geoff, Alex and georgie

First published in 1997 by
Sally Milner Publishing Pty Ltd
P.O. Box 2104
Bowral N.S.W. 2576
Australia

Reprinted 1999

Photography by Ben Wrigley, Canberra
Designed by Samantha Seery, ANU Graphics, Canberra
Printed and bound by National Capital Printing, Canberra

National Library of Australia Cataloguing-in-Publication data:

Cleary, Rhondda. Fragrant Candles : a practical guide to
making candles for the home and garden.

ISBN 1 86351 239 X

1. Candles.
2. Candlemaking. I. Title. (series : Milner craft series).

745.59332

ACKNOWLEDGEMENTS

I would like to acknowledge the following people and thank them for their assistance:

Sally Milner for suggesting I write this book

Ben Wrigley for his wonderful photographs

Dianne Summerhayes for her computing skills

Paulene Cairnduff for her creativity with outside candlesticks

Holly Prattis for all her help

Struan Thomson for flower arrangements

James Butler, Andrew Hallinan, Helen Stevens and all the staff of the Pialligo Plant Farm

Therese Buckley — Aromatherapist

Alan Aston — Crafted Fish

Jan Maghie — Ceramic vegetables

Potwork Orange — Ceramic head

Polyco Candles

Candle Craft

Redpaths Beekeeping Supplies

Artiana Imports

Inner Harmony

Hands at Work

All photographs were taken at Pialligo Plant Farm, Canberra, Australia

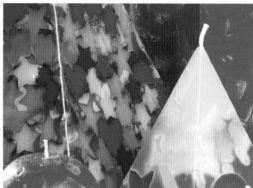

CONTENTS

part two
USING CANDLES IN THE HOME AND GARDEN

making your own candles

MAKING CANDLES

Generally speaking, the kitchen is the most suitable location for making candles. It has a heat source, water and work benches which make it safe as well as convenient.

However, the disadvantage is that making candles is a very messy occupation so you need to cover all your benches and the floor with newspaper, aluminium foil or brown paper.

Brown paper or aluminium foil is better because if you do spill wax it can be lifted once it is set and there will be no newsprint on it.

I have an outside table where I like to work on a fine day. I use a gas or a methylated spirits burner and I am not intimidated by the thought of spilling wax everywhere.

If you are going to take on candlemaking with a passion then you may want to set up a special area.

The essential ingredients for candlemaking—moulds, wicking, wax, stearic acid, thermometer, wick holders, colour buds, double boiler, skewer, wooden spoon, measuring jug, water bath, beeswax sheets.

EQUIPMENT

A HEAT SOURCE

The hotplates on your stove are most suitable, otherwise a temporary hot plate must be arranged.

A DOUBLE BOILER

Wax must never be put on a direct heat so therefore you need a double boiler. It is preferable that it be made of stainless steel or aluminium. Aluminium pots can be sourced very cheaply secondhand. I prefer the top of the double boiler to be an old coffee pot, glass jug (heatproof) or teapot, as it makes pouring the wax much easier. For making taper candles or dipping tall candles I use a tall container obtained from a catering supply company.

A WAX THERMOMETER

A candy or wax thermometer with a scale measuring 38°C (100°F)—100°C (212°F). Temperatures of wax are important when making candles so this needs to be accurate.

A SKEWER

This is used to poke into the candle as it sets to release air bubbles.

WOODEN SPOONS

These are necessary for stirring the wax and mixing the colour and stearic acid into it.

MEASURING JUG

This is for measuring the capacity of a mould— 450 grams of wax melts to a volume of approximately 1 litre. (1 lb of wax melts to a volume of approximately 2 pints.)

WATER BATH

You need a bucket or baking dish which is as tall as the mould so the mould is submerged to within 2.5 cms (1 inch) of the top. The bath is filled with warm water to ensure the candle has a smooth and shiny finish.

GREASEPROOF PAPER OR ALUMINIUM PAPER

This is used to line old containers for pouring excess wax. I store mine in a couple of old three-tier aluminium cake tins, each compartment holding a different colour.

PAPER TOWELS

Used for cleaning pots and cleaning up generally.

A METAL SPOON

Used for tapping the mould to release air bubbles.

OVEN MITS

For handling containers of hot wax.

A WEIGHT

I use a brick to weigh the mould down as it sits in the bucket.

SCISSORS

Needed for cutting wicks, masking tape and cutting wicks free from the bottom of the moulds.

A HAMMER

For breaking wax. I have an old pillowcase and put the slabs of wax in this and hit it with a hammer to break it into small pieces. This means the wax stays cleaner.

MASKING TAPE

Used to seal the wick hole so wax does not leak through the bottom of the moulds.

A FRYPAN

The candle is rubbed along the heel of the pan to level the bottom surface if necessary to ensure that it stands straight.

KITCHEN SCALES

Used for weighing wax.

SHARP KNIFE

For trimming candles.

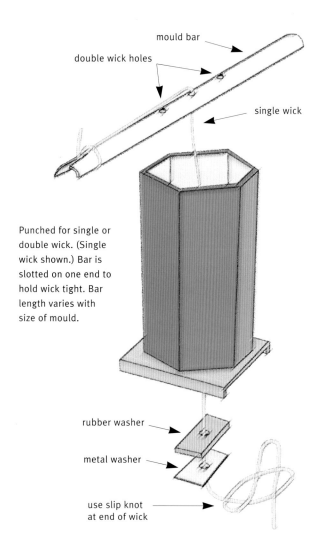

mould bar

double wick holes

single wick

Punched for single or double wick. (Single wick shown.) Bar is slotted on one end to hold wick tight. Bar length varies with size of mould.

rubber washer

metal washer

use slip knot at end of wick

MOULDS

A mould is a vessel that will contain the hot liquid wax and allow removal of the hardened wax. There is a great variety of commercial moulds on the market today. Metal moulds are perhaps the most popular. They come in many different shapes and usually come with a metal wick holder which sits on the top of the mould as well as a metal washer and a piece of rubber which seal the bottom of the mould. These moulds last a long time if looked after properly and will produce handsome, shiny candles. It is very important not to dent or scratch these moulds.

If there are residues of wax left in the mould they can be removed. First heat the oven to 170°C (338°F). Then place the mould upside down on a tray covered with alfoil. The wax will slide down the mould and collect on the foil.

Some moulds come equipped with a special 'wicker'. This is a reusable wicking device which can be used on metal or plastic moulds. It consists of a mould bar, a metal washer and a rubber washer.

To use these tie a slip knot at the lower end of the wick threading the other end through the metal washer then push it through the rubber washer with the point of a pencil. Then thread the wick through the hole in the bottom of the mould and through the centre hole in mould bar. Pull wick taut and insert wick in slot at end of mould bar. Wrap wick once around the mould bar, then through the slot to lock it in place.

If you do not have a wicker then the mould bar can be replaced by a pencil or a piece of dowelling and the washers can be replaced by the use of mould seal or masking tape. It is very very important to ensure that no wax leaks through this hole. If this does happen plunge the mould quickly into cold water and attempt to seal it properly.

There are plastic moulds which have two identical pieces which are taped together to form a three-dimensional mould. These must not be used with wax heated to more than 88°C (190°F). These moulds always come with good directions.

Rubber moulds are very strong one piece moulds and are often used by commercial candlemakers as they can be used many many times without damage to the mould. They can be the shape of a regular taper candle or a very sophisticated moulded shape and are often used for making beeswax candles.

There is also a good selection of glass moulds which, providing they are looked after, will have a good life.

HOMEFOUND MOULDS

Milk cartons, paper cups, ice cream containers, cardboard tubes, corrugated cardboard formed into shapes, glasses, cups — just look in your kitchen cupboard or in your recycle bin and you will find all sorts of moulds. Muffin tins or jelly moulds can always be put to use. The best moulds do not have seams and they must be strong enough to resist the heat and weight of the wax. Most of the cardboard moulds will only be used once.

When using cardboard moulds make sure that you reinforce any areas where leaks may occur or where the mould may become distorted. This is done by taping these areas with masking tape.

When making votive or container candles there are many different containers you can use. Glasses, vases, tins, terracotta or ceramic pots, in fact any container where you can visualise a candle burning. There are two ways to do this — one is to place a tealight in the container and the other is to make a candle in the container.

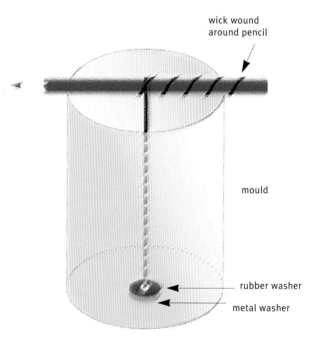

wick wound around pencil

mould

rubber washer

metal washer

INGREDIENTS

PARAFFIN WAX

Paraffin wax is a white, odourless, tasteless by-product of the oil-refining process and is the basis for most candlemaking. It is available in slabs or pellet form. Generally, candles are made of 90% paraffin wax and 10% stearic acid.

BEESWAX

Beeswax is a natural product from the hive with a sweet honey perfume. It is used in combination with paraffin wax to increase the burning time of the candle as well as to give the candle a rich yellow appearance, a honey perfume and a nice bright flame. Beeswax is much more expensive than paraffin wax but invaluable in making good candles. 10% of beeswax added to paraffin wax when making a candle makes for a much better candle. Modern church candles generally have 25% beeswax in their ingredients. You can use combinations of 50% paraffin wax and 50% beeswax or 70% paraffin, 10% beeswax and 20% stearic acid.

Sheets of beeswax come in a variety of colours including blue, red, green and natural. By rolling them, you can easily make the most wonderful candles.

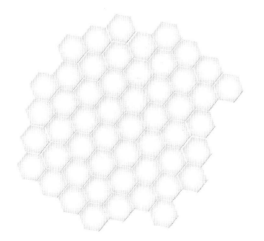

STEARIC ACID

Stearic acid is a white powder or granule derived from animal fat. 10% is added to paraffin wax when making a candle as it increases the shrinking quality to make release from the mould easier. It also makes the candle more opaque and intensifies the brightness of colour, lengthens the burning time and helps to stop the candle from dripping.

WICKS

Wicking is usually made of braided cotton which has been treated by chemicals to improve its burning qualities. Generally it comes in three sizes—small, medium and large.

Small wick should be used for candles up to 5 cms (2 inches) in diameter. Medium wick should be used for candles from 5 cms to 10 cms (2 inches to 4 inches) in diameter. Large wick should be used for candles from 10 cms to 15 cms (4 inches to 6 inches). For larger candles wicks should be plaited together to an appropriate size.

When you light the wick the wax melts and is absorbed into the wick and is burnt. The wick delivers the melted wax to the flame and vaporises into a burning gas.

Therefore, for a candle to burn correctly the wick must consume the melted wax as quickly as it accumulates. If the wick is too small the wax will not be absorbed quickly enough and the flame will be extinguished by the excess molten wax in the centre or the excess wax will drip down the sides of the candle. If the wick is too large the candle will smoke and, because it will absorb the melted wax faster than the flame can consume it, it will probably go out.

All the wicks must be primed before they can be used. This means giving them at least two coats of wax which has been melted to at least 77°C (170°F). Straighten and smooth it with your fingers as it dries. Do this firmly as any air pockets captured in the wick will cause the candles to spit as they burn.

CANDLE PERFUMES

There are two types available, both having oil bases.

First are the essential oils which are pure plant oils and have many therapeutic values. They are sold widely at stores with specialist aromatherapy areas and most retail outlets will have testers so you can work out which smell appeals to you the most.

The second type are the fragrant or synthetic oils, sometimes marked as candle oils, which are cheaper to buy but have no therapeutic qualities.

Commercial perfumes and colognes cannot be used as they have water or alcohol bases which are quite volatile and do not release any odour when burnt.

WAX DYES

Specially manufactured dyes for colouring candles are very effective and inexpensive to buy. They usually come in pellet or disc form and in a variety of colours. The primary colours can be mixed to achieve any colour you wish. Generally 20 grams of dye colours 2 kg wax (2/3 ounce to 4 lbs).

You need to experiment with the intensity of colour required—it is better to start with a little and build up your colour.

MOULD SEAL

A waterproof putty which is used to seal the bottom of makeshift moulds. It can be obtained from hardware stores, plumbing suppliers or craft shops.

MOULD RELEASE

The most effective is silicone spray which is sprayed lightly on the inside of the mould. Vegetable oil sprays also work well—however do not use olive oil as it forms a film on the outside of the candle.

HOW TO MAKE YOUR MOULDED CANDLE

Preparing the mould by inserting the primed wick through the wick holder

Adding stearic acid and colour to melted wax in double boiler

Pouring coloured, perfumed wax into the mould

1 Prepare the wax

Calculate the amount of wax you will need by filling your mould with water. For every 100 mls of water you will need 90 grams of cold wax (3 1/2 fluid ounces to 3 ounces). If your paraffin wax is in a slab put it in a bag or old pillowcase and break into smaller pieces with a hammer. Calculate amount required.

2 Prepare the wick

Calculate the length and width of the wick needed and then prime it by dipping in hot paraffin wax. Give it at least 2 coats of wax which have been melted to at least 77°C (170°F). Straighten or smooth it with your fingers to release any air pockets.

3 Prepare the mould

Lightly spray the inside of your mould with silicone spray or clear vegetable oil (not olive oil as it will leave a coating on the candle). Tie a slip knot at the lower end of the wick and thread through a metal washer and then a rubber washer with the point of a pencil.

Thread through hole at the bottom of the mould and then through hole of mould bar or else around pencil, pulling until taut and then attaching firmly to end of mould bar or pencil. Cover wick hole at bottom with masking tape or mould seal if not using washers.

4 Melt the wax

Weigh the wax. Put in the top of the double boiler and fill the bottom with water. Put the double boiler on the hot plate at 180°C (350°F). Put the thermometer in the wax.

5 Add additives

When the temperature of the wax reaches 93°C (200°F) add the stearic acid (10% of total wax) and the dyes—mix thoroughly. Use about 10 drops of oil to each 500 grams (approx 1lb) of wax. Add the essential oils at the very last so they don't 'cook'.

6 Pouring wax into mould

Fill a plastic bucket or other appropriate container with water to the height of the mould. Pour the liquid wax into the mould slowly allowing the wax to run down the inside of the mould to prevent the formation of air bubbles. Lightly tap the outside of the mould with a spoon once the candle is poured to also prevent bubbles forming on the outside of the candle. Place mould in water bath. Put a clean brick on the mould to stop it floating or tipping. The candle will begin to form as the wax hardens from the outside towards the centre.

Tapping the mould to release air bubbles

Immersing mould in water with weight on the top

Unmoulding finished candle

7 Refilling the mould

As the wax cools it shrinks and a large cavity forms in the top of the candle. After the candle has been in the water for approximately 40 minutes use a skewer to pierce the crust that has formed and push it down within 2 cms (1 inch) of the bottom of the candle. Remove the skewer and repeat three or four times close to the wick. Slowly pour wax (still at 93°C, 200°F) down these holes. It will probably be necessary to repeat this process at least once more. This releases the entrapped air and results in a candle which burns much more efficiently—be sure not to let the wax drip down the side of the candle as it will make it difficult to remove the candle from the mould and spoil the finish.

8 Cooling the candle

Leave the candle in the water bath for at least 3 hours. Remove the candle and let it set in the mould at room temperature for 8–10 hours.

9 Removing the candle from the mould

Remove the masking tape or mould seal or the nut and washer from the bottom of the mould and pull the wick at the bottom of the mould straight. The end of the wick will be the end that burns. Tip the mould and tap it gently to unmould the candle. If it doesn't slide out put it in the refrigerator for half an hour. If it still doesn't come out quickly apply some hot water to the outside of the mould. This should only be done in desperation as it spoils the finish of the candle. Never hit the mould as any indentations will make it impossible to remove the candle.

10 Finishing the candle

If the candle does not stand straight then rub it along the base of a warm frypan until it is level. If your candle has a seam from the mould, then use a fine knife or vegetable peeler to trim it. Polish the candle with an old piece of silk or a stocking.

If your mould has any wax residue left after you turn out the candle place the mould upside down in an oven to 88°C (215°F) on a tray covered with aluminium foil. The wax will run out onto the foil. Wipe clean.

COLOURING CANDLES

My first venture into candlemaking was because I wanted some bright orange candles and some bright green candles and some bright yellow candles. Even though there were many candles available commercially, there were none in these wonderful strong colours.

There are some excellent candlemaking dyes available — usually bought as discs, powders, pellets or sticks. They come in primary colours and so when you start making candles you only need to have red, blue and yellow dyes and by mixing you can have any colour you wish (except gold and silver). They are very concentrated and only a small amount is needed. 5–10 grams of colour will colour 500 grams of natural wax (1/4 – 1/2 ounce to 1 lb). Add small amounts and build the colour up as it is too late when you have put in too much. More dye does not necessarily mean better colour as it can often cause candles to look very dull.

And remember that colours lighten as the wax hardens.

It's a good idea to put a small amount of wax on a cupped piece of foil before you pour the candle and as it hardens it will give you a good idea of colour.

The following is a good guide to colouring candles:

White candle	add 20% stearic acid
Christmas red candle	7 grams of red dye to 500 grams wax (1/4 ounce to 1 lb)
Christmas green candle	3 grams of yellow and 3 grams blue dye to 500 grams wax (1/8 ounce plus 1/8 ounce to 1 lb)
Bright orange candle	5 grams of orange dye to 500 grams wax (1/5 ounce to 1 lb)
Lavender candle	2 grams of violet dye to 500 grams wax (1/10 ounce to 1 lb)

Brightly coloured candles have been perfumed
with a collection of exotic essential oils.

ESSENTIAL OILS AND CANDLES

The combination of essential oils and candles can truly enhance peace of mind and harmony in the environment. There can also be therapeutic benefits derived from their use. Life is not a dress rehearsal; make every moment count and enjoy something beautiful each day.

Essential oils are pure plant extracts whereas fragrant oils are artificially manufactured. You will notice that essential oils are more expensive than fragrant oils but nothing can compare with the fresh, natural aroma of essential oils, nor their personal and environmental benefits.

Essentials are identified by their labelling as it will always state 'ESSENTIAL OIL' on the bottle. If this is not present then you can assume it is a fragrant oil.

There are three ways to ensure you have fragrance in your candles.

1   The first is to make your own candles and add the essential oils to the hot wax just before you pour into the mould. This means you get exactly the perfumes you desire.

    Votive candles are very good to perfume as you can put as much oil in as you wish and it will not harm the structure of the candle. We have to be a little bit careful with a moulded candle as too much oil will make the candle mottled.

    Generally speaking, a candle which uses 500 grams (approx 1 lb) of wax should have about 10 drops of essential oil. It is usually best to use combinations of up to 3 essential oils at a time—more than this gets a bit confusing.

2   The second way to create a perfumed candle is to add oils to a purchased candle. Place 4-12 drops of your favourite oils on the melted candle wax (depending on the size of the candle) and then re-light. These oils will be more volatile so if they fade then just add more. It is preferable to add oils to the candle when it is not alight as the oils can be flammable.

3   The third way is to purchase candles which are already impregnated with oils. There are some superb perfumed candles available for sale and let your nose dictate what you should buy. Once you have used essential oils you will probably find you prefer their fresh natural smell to the synthetic oils sometimes used in candles and you will be able to tell the difference.

I find I use specific oils to create different mood spaces. For instance, I always burn basil (for concentration) or rosemary (for remembrance) in my work space and so there is no way I would burn these oils when I am wanting to relax as to me the perfume immediately evokes a sense of concentration and discipline.

I burn lavender when I want to relax and wind down whereas when I entertain I like to use citrus oils like lime, mandarin, orange and tangerine and because I just adore the smell of frankincense I add this wherever possible. In our classroom lemongrass is the most requested.

fragrant candles

AROMATHERAPY

Aromatherapy, or aromaessence as I prefer to call it, is a healing art with a tradition dating back thousands of years. And yet it is one of the most popular of the modern natural therapies, incorporating the pleasing benefits of touch and smell. Aromaessence uses essential oils, highly aromatic pure plant extracts; these essences awaken our spirit. Aromatherapy is a truly holistic therapy having a powerful effect on the mind, the body and the spirit.

The aroma of essential oils is very powerful. We are mostly unaware of our scentual environment, but odours are capable of triggering memories or emotional responses. Our olfactory nerve is an extension of the brain itself. An odour can stimulate centres of the brain which can result in the release of hormones or neurotransmitters. Thus, simply inhaling the aromas of essential oils can trigger emotional responses, or create the feeling of relaxation, euphoria or stimulation, and can even affect the physical functioning of our body.

Sometimes, after ten or fifteen minutes, the scent of the oils may fade as the olfactory cells are full. However, as they empty and refill the perfume comes back again.

ENVIRONMENTAL FRAGRANCING WITH ESSENTIAL OILS

One of the most beautiful and effective ways of fragrancing your environment with essential oils is the use of a candle burner. A candle burner uses a tealight candle to warm a crucible of water to which a number of drops of essential oil has been added. A tealight candle is a small candle in an aluminium container which should burn for about 8 hours. However, beware—there are many cheap varieties available which burn for as little as an hour. As the water is warmed tiny droplets of essential oil evaporate with the water, to create an aromatic and harmonious environment.

Candle burners are available in a wide range of designs to suit personal tastes and decor. They are completely silent in operation and the flickering light of the candle creates a mood and beauty which enhances the atmosphere created by the aromas of the essential oils. Candle burners are ideal for dinner parties, meditation, candle-lit rejuvenating baths or for simply creating an atmosphere of peace and harmony in the home or workplace.

When choosing your candle burner, be sure that the design conforms to the applicable safety standards. When choosing ceramic models, the glazing should be of a quality that does not chip or crack with repeated uses. In all cases, there should be sufficient distance between the candle and the crucible so that the water does not boil away too rapidly and the crucible should be of sufficient size so that it takes at least 3–4 hours for the water to completely evaporate.

It is important to choose a good quality tealight candle. Poor quality candles can melt rapidly creating a hazard and mess. They may also burn with too great a heat causing

Aromatherapy burner with tea-light candle.

the water in the crucible to boil rapidly away. Some tealight candles are carbonless; this means they will not create the blackening that can mar the beauty of your candle burner.

To Use Your Candle Burner:
First fill the crucible with water. Add the required drops of essential oil to the water. For a burner that operates for 3–4 hours, use approximately 4 drops of essential oil. For a larger capacity burner that can operate for 8–12 hours, use 9–12 drops of essential oil. Place the burner on a stable surface away from drafts and children, and light the candle.

MOOD ENHANCING CANDLES

These are some suggested oils to use in your candles for creating a special ambience.

Study and Concentration	Rosemary, Basil, Lemon, Peppermint, Black Pepper
Meditation	Frankincense, Myrrh, Sandalwood
To Encourage Sleep	Bergamot, Lavender, Marjoram, Chamomile, Orange
Romance and Intimacy	Rose, Neroli, Ylang Ylang, Jasmine, Patchouli, Clary, Sage
Celebrations and Parties	Orange, Geranium, Frankincense
Peace and Harmony	Lavender, Rose, Sandalwood, Chamomile, Vetiver, Bergamot, Boronia
Christmas	Frankincense, Myrrh, Orange, Cedarwood, Pine, Black Pepper, Ginger, Clove
Purifying and Cleansing	Rosemary, Eucalyptus, Juniper, Lemon, Lemongrass, Pine, Teatree
Invigorating	Cardamon, Juniper, Lemongrass, Rosemary
Nausea	Spearmint, Peppermint, Ginger

NB: Use combinations of up to 3 oils only as more than 3 is too confusing

USING CARDBOARD MOULDS

Cardboard rolls such as those found inside paper towels make very good candle moulds. Have a look in your kitchen cupboard or maybe next time you are in the supermarket, have a look for good shapes and sizes. I have found I have used some of them many times over. Corrugated cardboard is also good—it gives a lovely striped texture to the candle.

To make the corrugated cardboard mould, cut to size allowing approximately 2 cms (1 inch) overlap and then spray inside with silicone spray or vegetable oil. Tape the sides with very strong masking tape or double sided tape.

Equipment

Double boiler

Cardboard mould
and bottom

Wick holder
and washer

Thermometer

Mould seal

Silicone spray or
vegetable oil

Skewer

Wooden spoon

Scales

Scissors

Ingredients

Paraffin wax

Stearic acid

Primed wick

Candle dye

Candle perfume

HOW TO MAKE THE CANDLES

1   Place the mould over a makeshift bottom—e.g. a plastic lid or heavy cardboard.

2   Make the mould absolutely waterproof by sealing with mould seal where necessary.

3   Spray inside with silicone spray or vegetable oil.

4   Make a hole in middle of bottom of candle mould.

5   Prepare mould as for moulded candle.

6   Heat paraffin wax (with 10% stearic acid) to 84°C (180°F).

7   Pour into mould.

8   As the candle starts to set insert skewer into candle near wick 3 or 4 times and refill.

9   When candle has cooled either break mould away or remove as for normal moulded candle.

NB: The wax is heated to a lower temperature than a normal moulded candle.

STRIPED CANDLES

The photograph here shows wonderful striped candles in very bright colours which match my dining table setting. These make for a very joyful and happy environment.

My first experiment making a moulded striped candle was a disaster as I thought I would use my leftover wax each time I made a candle and create this wonderful striped candle. So, away I went, poured my first layer, a couple of days later my second layer and by the time I got to my fifth layer some days later I realised that none of these layers were sticking together. The only common bond was the wick down the centre. Another lesson learnt. I now have the greatest respect for the striped candle. The layers must be poured approximately 60 minutes apart so each adheres to the previous layer.

Equipment

Double boiler

Candle mould

Wick holder
and washer

Thermometer

Silicone spray

Skewer

Wooden spoon

Scales

Water bath

Weight

Scissors

Sharp knife

Saucepans

Ingredients

Paraffin wax

Stearic acid

Wick

Candle dye

Essential oils

HOW TO MAKE THE CANDLES

1   Set up your candle mould (see Moulded Candles, page 14).

2   Have several saucepans each with equal amounts of wax if you want equal stripes or different amounts for different size stripes. Add 10% stearic acid, dye and then add essential oils just before you pour.

3   Heat the paraffin wax for the first stripe to 91°C (195°F)and pour into mould. Place mould into a water bath for a few minutes, then remove and leave for approximately 45 minutes. Puncture candle and refill with wax as you would for a normal candle. Leave until a firm, warm skin has formed on the top.

4   Pour the next layer. Immerse in water again. Puncture and refill. Do not let the wax harden or the layers will not fuse together. Pour each layer into the centre of the candle being careful not to drizzle down the side of the mould.

5   When ready, unmould candle as normal. If any wax has seeped down the side of the candle trim with a sharp knife and polish candle with a piece of silk or stocking.

6   To make the stripes slanted tilt the mould slightly on its side so that the wax sets on a slant. Each layer could be set at a different angle. The last layer must be poured with the mould standing straight.

7   To avoid using lots of saucepans you could work with shades starting with a lighter colour, progressively adding more dye to obtain darker shades.

Striped candles co-ordinating the rich jewel colours in my dining room.

MOSAIC CANDLES

Mosaic candles are full of chunks of different colours and shapes and apart from their wonderful artistic appearance, it is a good way to use leftover wax.

This photograph shows a wonderful variety of sizes and colours of mosaic candles.

The first thing to do is to make the interesting shapes to form the mosaics. This can be as simple as setting wax in an iceblock container. However, I like to take a baking pan, line it with foil and pour in the coloured melted wax to a depth of approximately 5 cms (2 inches). I have preheated the wax to 93°C (200°F) and added a little more stearic acid for hardness.

Once the wax has cooled but is still pliable I cut it into shapes with a sharp knife or a scalpel. Cut red hearts or perhaps pink pigs with a biscuit cutter. Mosaic candles look great with lots of different shapes and colours.

Equipment

Double boiler

Candle mould

Wick holder and washer

Thermometer

Silicone spray

Skewer

Wooden spoon

Metal spoon

Scales

Water bath

Weight

Scissors

Ingredients

Paraffin wax

Chunks of wax

Stearic acid

Primed wick

Candle dye

Essential oils

HOW TO MAKE THE CANDLES

1   Place wick in mould as for moulded candle. (See Moulded Candles, page 14.)

2   Melt the light coloured paraffin wax and 10% stearic acid wax to 82°C (180°F). Add essential oils. Don't make the wax any hotter or it will melt the chunks.

3   Arrange blocks in the mould taking care not to shift the wick.

4   Pour the wax into the mould.

5   Place the candle in a water bath.

6   Puncture the candle and refill.

7   Unmould as normal.

A wonderful collection of mosaic and striped candles in many colours.

ICE CANDLES

Ice candles look like Swiss cheese. With a bit of imagination they can be coloured yellow and used as a table centrepiece. Maybe add a mouse or two (not live!!).

You will need a tray of ice cubes or some crushed ice for a less dramatic effect. The other more unusual ingredient is a taper candle as this will be used instead of a wick because if the wick gets wet the candle will not burn.

Equipment

Double boiler

Candle mould

Wick holder and washer

Thermometer

Silicone spray

Skewer

Wooden spoon

Scales

Scissors

Ingredients

Paraffin wax

Stearic acid

Made Taper candle

Candle dye

Ice cubes

HOW TO MAKE THE CANDLES

1   Prepare the mould (see Moulded Candles, page 14) but instead of inserting a wick, insert the taper candle with the wick out the wick hole. Seal hole with masking tape or mould seal.

2   Melt the wax to 93°C (200°F) and add the stearic acid, dye and lastly the essential oils. Break up ice if necessary and then place in mould so the taper candle is standing straight.

3   Pour the wax into the mould amongst the ice cubes.

4   When the wax has hardened release the candle from the mould and the ice which, of course, will have melted, and drain away.

5   Make sure you completely dry the mould so it does not rust.

A variation is to pour another colour of wax into the mould after the water has drained away, creating an unusual colour combination.

Collection of candles (clockwise from left): Hurricane candle, Ice candle, Stencilled candle, Pressed flower candle, Glow candle, Painted candle and bunch of cardboard moulded candles on inside.

GLOW CANDLES

These candles are very romantic but easy to make. They are simply candles where the flame shines through the translucent walls of pure paraffin, producing a glow.

Don't use stearic acid when preparing the wax for this candle as the candle needs to be translucent.

Also use a slightly finer wick than usual as this will cause the candle to burn down the centre.

Equipment

Double boiler

Candle mould

Wick holder
and washer

Thermometer

Silicone spray

Skewer

Wooden spoon

Scales

Water bath

Weight

Scissors

Ingredients

Paraffin wax

Wick

Candle dye

Essential oils

HOW TO MAKE THE CANDLES

1   Prepare the mould and wick as for a Moulded Candle (page 14) making sure the mould is well oiled as with no stearic acid there will be little shrinkage. Use a finer wick than normal.

2   Heat the required paraffin wax to 82°C (180°F) — add dye, mix and then add essential oils.

3   Pour wax into mould and place in water bath.

4   Puncture and refill.

5   Unmould as normal.

HURRICANE CANDLES

You are well-rewarded when you make a hurricane candle because it does not burn away.

A hurricane candle is a hollow shell of wax inside which sits a tea light or a votive candle—it is more like a lantern. We do not use stearic acid in the wax as the walls need to be translucent so the light can shine through.

These days there are special moulds made with the outside mould not having a hole for a wick and the slightly smaller inside mould just being a metal shell with no bottom. However, if you do not have a special mould there is a way of improvising.

Equipment

Double boiler

Candle mould

Thermometer

Ladle

Sharp knife

Wooden spoon

Scissors

Ingredients

Paraffin wax

Candle dye

Essential oils

HOW TO MAKE THE CANDLES

1   Take a normal mould which is at least 10cm (4 inches) in diameter. Close the wick hole with mould seal so wax does not leak through.

2   Oil the mould.

3   Heat the paraffin to 91°C (195°F) and pour it into the mould.

4   Place in water bath and weigh down.

5   When a film of wax 3mm (1/8 inch) thick forms across the top and the sides are set to a thickness of approximately 6mm (1/4 inch), insert a knife 10mm (1/3 inch) from the edge and cut out the top layer. Remove all liquid wax from the centre of the mould with a ladle.

6   When the shell has completely hardened remove from the mould and gently cut out the base section with a sharp knife.

7   The top can be levelled off by rubbing over a warm frypan.

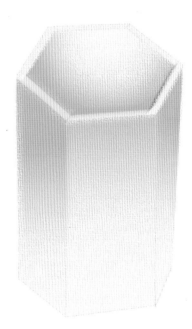

CANDLES WITH PRESSED FLOWERS

Candles decorated with pressed flowers can look quite stunning although I have to confess I've never had the courage to burn one. It seems a pity to go to all that trouble to press the flowers and then to arrange them on the candle, only to see them go up in smoke.

The candles make lovely gifts and essential oils can be added later to match the flowers decorating the candles. For example, a candle decorated with lavender flowers can have lavender essential oil added to it.

Equipment

Double boiler

Tweezers

Tea towel

Teaspoon

Ingredients

Made candle

Pressed or dried flowers

Paraffin wax

Florigraphy was very popular in Victorian times. It was a way of sending hidden messages and adding nuances by changing the placement of the flowers. A full blown rose placed over two buds means secrecy but when inverted it means the opposite.

You might like to make a candle for someone special by using your own language of flowers (see opposite).

HOW TO MAKE THE CANDLES

1   Place the candle on a folded tea towel to prevent it from slipping.

2   Dip a metal teaspoon in a cup of boiling water.

3   Rub the back of the spoon where you want the first pressed flower to be placed.

4   Using tweezers place the flower and press gently into the candle until it adheres.

If the candle is large you may wish to place the flowers on paper beforehand to create a pattern. However, it generally can be done by 'eye'. It is advisable to create the main pattern at the bottom of the candle so it will last longer when the candle burns.

When you are happy with the decoration heat plain paraffin wax in a double boiler to 88°C (190°F). Using tweezers dip the candle in wax for about 4 seconds, then remove. Dip as many times as necessary for the required finish.

THE LANGUAGE OF FLOWERS

Acacia
secret love

Almond blossom
hope

Amaryllis
pride, splendid beauty

Anemone
forsaken

Apple blossom
preference

Bell flower, white
gratitude

Bluebell
constancy

Broom
humility

Camellia, red
unpretending excellence

Camellia, white
perfected excellence

Carnation, red
alas for my poor heart

Carnation, striped
refusal

Chamomile
patience

Chrysanthemum, red
I love

Clematis
mental beauty, purity

Columbine
folly

Daisy
innocence

Elderflower
compassion, consolation

Everlasting flower
unfading memory

Forget-me-not
fidelity, true love

Hawthorn blossom
hope

Heartsease
remembrance

Hibiscus
delicate beauty

Honeysuckle
devotion

Hyacinth
unobtrusive loveliness

Hyacinth, blue
constancy

Jasmine, white
amiability

Jasmine, yellow
happiness, grace
& elegance

Jonquil
I desire a return
of affection

Lavender
silence

Lilac, purple
first emotions of love

Lilac, white
youthful innocence

Lily
purity

Lily of the valley
purity, return of
happiness

Magnolia
grief

Marigold
joy

Michaelmas daisy
farewell

Mignonette
your qualities
are supreme

Nasturtium
patriotism

Orange blossom
purity and loveliness

Pansies
love, thought

Peony
bashfulness

Pinks
love

Poppy, red
consolation

Primrose
early youth

Rose
love

Rose, musk
capricious beauty

Rosebud
pure and lovely

Rosemary
remembrance

Snowdrop
hope

Stock
lasting beauty

Sweet William
gallantry

Tulip
love

Violet
modesty

Wallflower
fidelity in adversity

Zinnia
thoughts of
absent friends

fragrant candles

33

fLOATING CANDLES

Floating candles are simple to use and simple to make. This photograph shows floating candles in the shape of a sunflower floating on our fish pond. They can be floated in a tiny bowl or in a swimming pool.

Hunt around the kitchen shops for moulds—metal 'petit four' tins make ideal moulds. They come in all shapes from fish to flowers or stars to shells. Just use your imagination. The main criteria is that the mould will float.

Equipment

Double boiler

Moulds

Thermometer

Vegetable oil

Wooden spoon

Scissors

Skewer

Ingredients

Paraffin wax

Stearic acid

Primed wick

Candle dyes

Essential oils

HOW TO MAKE THE CANDLES

1   Melt the paraffin wax and add 10% stearic acid and dye. Heat to 82°C (180°F).

2   Add essential oils.

3   Pour into moulds which have been lightly brushed with vegetable oil.

4   Place moulds in shallow water in a pan, weighing them down if necessary.

5   When wax is setting it will shrink in the centre so top up with more wax melted to 82°C (180°F).

6   Unmould when set.

7   Upturn moulded candle and pierce a hole in the centre of each shape with a heated skewer.

8   Insert wick and top up with more wax if necessary.

Lovely floating candles in the shape and colour of sunflowers in my fish pond.

CANDLES EMBEDDED WITH SHELLS

These candles are most charming and any assortment of embellishments can be used so long as they can take the heat of the wax. You may like to use beads, fake flowers, dried flowers, leaves, gold cherubs, all sorts of things.

Equipment

Double boiler

Candle mould

Wick holder and washer

Thermometer

Silicone spray

Skewer

Wooden spoon

Scales

Water bath

Weight

Ingredients

Paraffin wax

Stearic acid

Primed wick

Candle dye

Essential oils

Shells

HOW TO MAKE THE CANDLES

1   Prepare the mould as normal, inserting the wick.

2   Melt the wax to 93°C (200°F) and add the stearic acid, dye and lastly the essential oils.

3   Lay the mould on its side and arrange the shells as you wish to see them on the side of the candle.

4   Carefully spoon the wax over the objects without moving them. Let the wax set and then gradually organise each side of the mould.

5   When the outer shell is established carefully fill the mould with wax.

6   Cool in water bath.

7   Puncture candle and refill.

8   Unmould as normal.

*Candles embedded with seashells
and other dried sea creatures.*

PAINTED CANDLES

Painted candles are such fun to make and a great exercise for children. They are wonderful for theme parties or alternatively they can be used to match a particular decor.

One of my friends collects frogs (not live ones!) and she always paints little naive frogs on her candles. The frogs change according to the occasion—at Christmas she has Santa frogs and at Easter she has a frog sitting in an egg. I now have a special collection of these candles which I have saved over the years and there is no way I will ever burn one.

Equipment

Double boiler

Acrylic paints

Artist's brush

Dishwashing liquid

Ingredients

Made candles

Paraffin wax

HOW TO MAKE THE CANDLES

1 Clean the surface of the candle so there is no dust on it.

2 Mix the paint with a little dishwashing liquid to make it a smooth consistency.

3 Apply paint to candle.

4 Melt paraffin wax in double boiler to 88°C (190°F).

5 Holding the candle by the wick with tweezers, dip the candle into the wax for about 3 seconds so a coating has formed over the painting.

6 It can be dipped as many times as you wish, keeping in mind that the clarity will diminish with more coats.

STENCILLING CANDLES

Stencilled candles are simple to make and a very ordinary candle can be turned into a work of art using this simple technique.

Recently, when my friends celebrated their 50th wedding anniversary, we took some big fat ivory beeswax candles and stencilled them with gold stars. We then tied gold bows of wired ribbon around them with long tails drifting down the centre of the table and sprinkled gold stars over the white cloth.

When the candles were burning the effect was magic.

Equipment

Double boiler

Stencil

Poster paint
or gouache

Masking tape

Small sponge

Dishwashing liquid

Ingredients

Made candles

Paraffin wax

HOW TO MAKE THE CANDLES

1   Tape stencil to candle firmly with masking tape.

2   Mix the paint with a little dishwashing liquid until quite thick.

3   Dab the paint onto the stencil with the sponge.

4   When dry, carefully remove the stencil.

5   Melt paraffin wax in double boiler to 88°C (190°F).

6   Holding the candle by the wick with tweezers, dip the candle into the wax for about 3 seconds so a coating has formed over the stencilling.

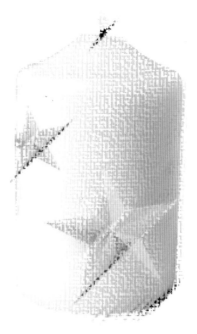

(DIPPED) TAPER CANDLES

Making taper candles requires a lot of patience but it is a lot of fun. I have made a collection of these in the colours of the rainbow and rather than burn them and see my work go up in smoke, I have them hanging over a gate which hangs in my living area.

To make these candles you will need a double boiler with the inside metal container being tall enough to accommodate the length of the candle required. Catering companies are often the best source of these. A container which is 30 cms (12 inches) high and 15 cms (6 inches) in diameter will hold about 3 kgs (6 lbs) of wax. This takes quite a time to melt so you may like to make several pairs at a time.

It is best to use uncoloured wax for most of the dips and use coloured wax for the last few dips—this will give a more intense colour.

To make these candles we use wax which is melted to a lower temperature 70°C (160°F) because if the temperature is higher it melts each previous layer of wax and so imperfections form on the side of the candle. However, if the wax is too cold, bubbles will form on the surface.

Equipment
Double boiler
Thermometer
Wooden spoon
Scissors
Broom handle
Newspaper

Ingredients
Paraffin wax
Primed wick
Metal nuts
Essential oils
Wax dyes

HOW TO MAKE THE CANDLES

1   Melt paraffin wax in a double boiler.

2   While this is melting, prepare your wick—measure a length of fine wick which is twice the length of your desired candle plus approximately 8cms (3 inches) for holding in the middle. I like to tie a small metal nut at each end to weigh it down and keep it straight.

3   Add colour and essential oils to wax or you can use natural colour and add colour for the last couple of dips.

4   Test wax temperature at 70°C (160°F) and prime the wick by dipping it into the wax up to the desired length of the candle for about 3 seconds, holding the wick at mid-point. Redip and then plunge it into cool water. When dry, redip again—repeat this process until the desired size of candle is reached—this may take 25–40 dips.

5   I hang finished candles over a broom handle strung between 2 chairs, placing newspaper underneath.

6   After a day or so cut weights off the bottom of the candles, trim the bases and redip in wax which has been heated to 82°C (180°F) so as to give them a smooth surface.

Coloured taper candles which I use as a decoration on an old gate hanging in my living room.

VOTIVE CANDLES

Votive candles are candles which are not removed from the moulds. Votive candles can be refilled with wax and used again and again. These candles can have as much essential oil added as you wish. With normal candles the addition of too much oil makes the wax liquid but because these candles are in containers this is not a problem.

These candles make wonderful gifts and are a great way to use leftover wax as well as using recycled containers.

A row of little candles looks wonderful on a mantelpiece, windowsill or table. Terracotta pots, thick glasses, old tins, cups with saucers—you are limited only by your imagination. A terracotta pot is transformed by spraying the inside with gold which creates wonderful reflections.

Equipment
Double boiler

Containers for candles

Thermometer

Skewer

Wooden spoon

Ingredients
Candle wax

Primed candle wicks

Candle dyes

Essential oils

One of my favourite votives is a glass container, with rows of cinnamon sticks glued on to cover the outside, tied with a raffia bow. I then place a tealight in the centre with a couple of drops of cinnamon oil on the melted wax. I like to burn these in the winter and place them next to my bowls of winter pot pourri which are full of cinnamon and oranges.

HOW TO MAKE THE CANDLES

1   If the container has a hole in the bottom, close with a piece of aluminium foil. I tend not to use stearic acid in these pots as we don't particularly want the candle to shrink from the pot. If I'm feeling really extravagant I will use lots of beeswax for longer burning and also for the wonderful beeswax perfume.

2   To calculate the amount of wax required fill the container with water.

3   Heat the wax to 90°C (195°F). Add the colour and you must add essential oils as votive candles need to smell wonderful.

4   If the candles are to be outside you might like to add citronella oil.

5   If the containers are breakable, make sure you heat them before pouring in the hot wax.

6   Once the wax has been poured and cooled, drill a hole into the candle and place the appropriately sized and primed wick. This can also be done by using a hot wire or skewer. Fill space around wick with hot wax.

7   The other way is to take the primed wick, tie a weight to one end (I use a metal nut), attach it to the bottom of the container with some florist or plumbers putty, and attach it to the bar or pencil across the top of the mould (see Moulded Candle, page 14).

fragrant candles

*Little teacup votive candles in my house—
I love to use these as individual table arrangements.*

BEESWAX CANDLES

Nothing surpasses the wonderful burning qualities and aroma of a beeswax candle. Beeswax is quite a lot more expensive than paraffin wax but well worth the extra cost if you want a high quality candle.

Beeswax candles are one of man's earliest sources of reliable light. The gentle flickers radiating from the flame of a beeswax candle have shone over more time than has the radiance of the electric light bulb. In fact, in Spanish cave paintings up to 9000 years old, man has been shown chasing bees for their honey and beeswax.

Beeswax has been used in diverse ways through the ages, from such things as simple candles during the Mesolithic time (8000 to 3000 B.C.) to Aristophanes, in (400 B.C.) having reportedly said that 'beeswax is good for many purposes, among which are metal protection, modelling, writing tablets and for sealing love letters'. During the Middle Ages many religious orders kept bees specifically for the production of honey and beeswax so they would have wax for candles and honey to make mead. In modern times we still use beeswax for so many diverse purposes including cosmetics, armaments, thread waxing, saddlery, archery, margarine stabilization and, of course, candles.

Today, the old time methods used to make beeswax candles are being rediscovered and enjoyed.

BEESWAX

Beeswax is a liquid formed in the wax glands on the underbelly of the honeybee. As it is exuded from the bee and comes into contact with air it solidifies. The bee then manipulates the flakes with its mandibles into the shape of honeycomb.

At this stage the beeswax is white or opaque, but within a short time, it will soon change to its natural yellow colour. The primary source of this colour change comes from the staining effect of pollen and propolis, thus causing its distinctive colour and aroma.

It is believed that beeswax is made up of more than 300 individual components and a breakdown of these leaves us with a mixture of Hydrocarbons 14%, Monoesters 35%, Diesters 14%, Triesters 3%, Hydroxy Monoesters 4%, Hydroxy Polyesters 8%, Acid Esters 1%, Acid Polyesters 2%, Free Acids 12%, Free Alcohols 1% and unidentified material 6%. These natural ingredients make it a wonderful choice for candles, providing it with a high melting point, so it burns longer, also leaving a lovely natural aroma.

Beeswax candles in the fireplace.

ROLLED BEESWAX CANDLES

I was rather surprised when looking for beeswax sheets for making rolled candles to find that many of these sheets are not beeswax at all. The best test for authenticity is the smell. Beeswax candles smell of luscious honey and are also quite sticky to touch. They are available in a natural colour and also blue, red and green—the latter two being wonderful for Christmas. These candles have the fragrance of honey when burning, and, remember—the fatter the candle, the longer it burns.

The candles in the photograph opposite were made with varying numbers of sheets of beeswax—some rolled on the short sides and some rolled on the long sides. Some are made with one sheet and the fattest candles with five or six sheets. These were made for Christmas and were tied with a stunning variety of Christmas ribbons.

A bunch of 3 small candles tied with a luscious ribbon makes a wonderful gift or just lying across a shelf or table it makes a lovely decoration.

I also find the beeswax a wonderful way to make a candle to fit a particular candle holder. For example, the Choir boys on page 58 require very thin candles which are bigger than normal birthday candles but smaller than other commercial candles. I just use a very fine wick and roll tiny beeswax candles to fit the hole—it works perfectly.

These beeswax candles are a pure delight to make and a very nice exercise for children. One sheet of beeswax can make many candles for a birthday cake.

Equipment
Paper or card

Sharp knife

Ingredients
Sheets of rolled beeswax

Primed wick

For Christmas candles try rolling one sheet of red beeswax and then over that roll 1 sheet of green beeswax. Make spiral candles by cutting beeswax into triangles before rolling. Place wick along the longer edge and roll towards the shorter edge. Two colour spirals can be made by using triangles of contrast-ing colours. See diagrams on page 49 for methods of rolling beeswax.

HOW TO MAKE THE CANDLES

1 Use paper or card to determine size of candles if necessary.

2 Place shape on beeswax sheet and cut carefully with a sharp knife. To increase thickness add more sheets.

3 Cut a piece of primed wick 2cm (1 inch) longer than the finished candle will be.

4 To soften beeswax wave hairdryer over sheet for a few seconds.

5 Lay sheet on a clean surface with wick along edge.

6 Using palms of both hands firmly roll wax away from you with a firm but even pressure, making sure that the candle is even. If air is trapped between the sheets then the candle will not burn evenly.

7 Press the outside of the wax against the candle to prevent it from unrolling.

8 Trim the wick to 1.5cm (1/2 inch) and pinch a piece of reserved wax around the base of the wick.

A collection of beeswax rolled candles decorated with ribbons and cherubs and ready for Christmas.

OTHER BEESWAX CANDLES

Dipped Candles

One of the earliest types of beeswax candles were ones dipped from a dipping tank of wax.

Follow the same instructions as for making a Dipped Candle on page 41, substituting beeswax for paraffin wax.

After the first dip allow to cool while straight, then dip again. It is best to straighten the candle on about the third dip then let it cool for a reasonable period before dipping many more times to gain the desired thickness. This will ensure you end up with a straight candle.

Cast Candles

These can be made quite easily if you have a suitable mould. A good simple mould is a straight PVC plastic plumbing pipe cut to a suitable length. Coat inside with a fine layer of silicone spray. It is a good idea to use a thicker wick than normal.

Equipment

Double boiler

Mould

Silicone spray

Box of fine sand

2 thin wooden rods
(butchers' skewers
are good)

Rubber bands

Ingredients

Beeswax

Wick

HOW TO MAKE THE CANDLES

1   Thread a wick of correct size down the mould and press tube vertically in a box of fine sand to hold mould straight.

2   To hold the wick in the centre of the tube at the top, make a bar from the two thin wooden rods. Hold the two rods together with rubber bands then thread the wick between the 2 rods.

3   Pull the excess wick through until tight and rods sit on top of tube.

4   Heat beeswax in double boiler to 70°C (160°F) and pour into mould.

5   Remove from mould when cool. If you have trouble releasing candle place in freezer for a while and this will cause beeswax to shrink slightly.

Available now, also, are high grade solid silicone rubber moulds, in over 150 various shapes and sizes and I should point out that these moulds are nothing like the plaster of Paris moulds we used as kids and then peeled off.

These moulds are extremely easy to use and long lasting. The wick is placed in the mould in a similar manner to that described above, using the two thin skewer rods to hold it and then the beeswax is poured in.

The beeswax never sticks to the silicone rubber so that when the candle has cooled, the mould can be easily split down one side allowing the candle to be eased out without damaging the finished candle.

Once finished, the candle may be painted, if desired, to make it much more than just a candle.

PARAFFIN WAX SHEETS

If you don't wish to be bothered by finding moulds and going to all the trouble of making a moulded candle, then there is a simpler solution.

You can make your own wax sheets and roll your candles. This is done by melting the paraffin wax in a double boiler to 70°C (185°F). Then add 10% stearic acid, the dye and the essential oils. Line a baking dish, or something similar, with aluminium foil taking care to tidy the corners.

Pour the wax in to a height of approximately 2−3 mms (1/10−1/8 inch) and let set. When you have made the desired number of sheets they can simply be stored by placing a sheet of foil or baking paper between them.

To make the candles simply soften by wafting the warm air of an electric hairdryer over them and then treat as for making a rolled beeswax candle. (See page 47.)

To give these candles a really professional finish you may like to dip in natural paraffin wax which has been heated to 93°C (225°F) in a double boiler.

These sheets can also be used for cutting out shapes to decorate a candle.

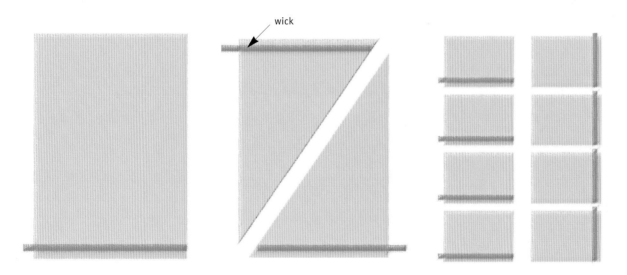

wick

Hand made beeswax or paraffin sheets can be trimmed to make different sized and shaped rolled candles.

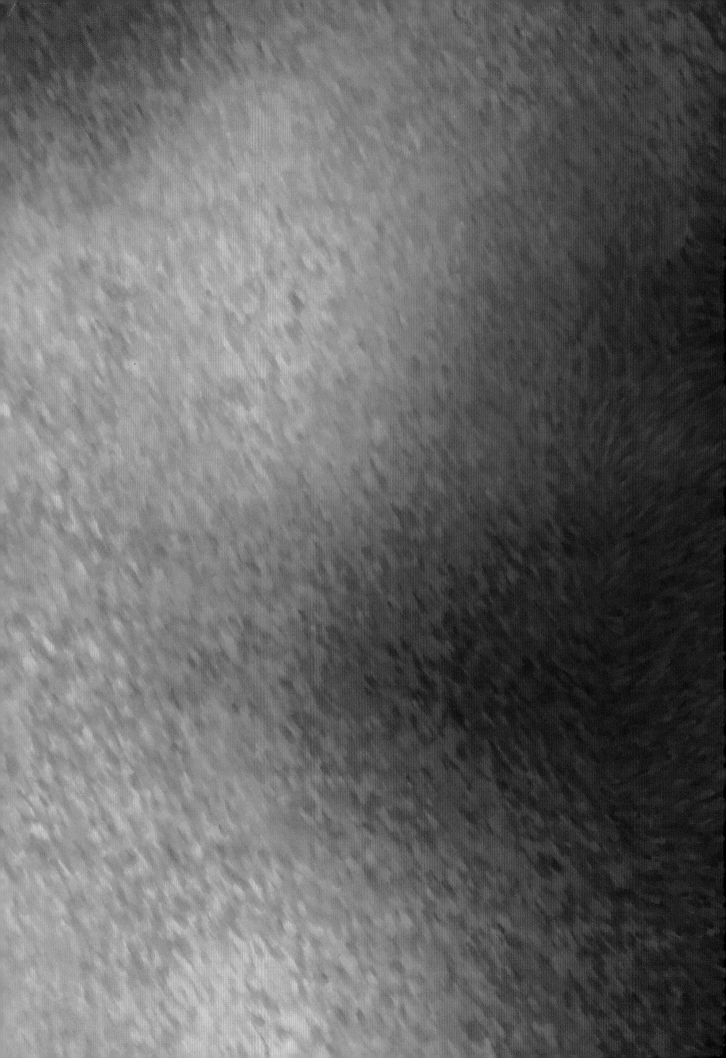

using candles in the home & garden

SOME DECORATIVE IDEAS

CANDLES AND GLASS

Our house has many ceiling to floor windows and I love to have heaps of candles alight on special occasions at night so that there are lots of reflections, making it appear as though there are many more candles than there really are. If placed carefully you can have four or five candles for the price of one. Candles can also be placed on the outside of the windows too, giving a very mysterious look.

A row of votive candles on a windowsill gives an interesting effect. If placed in glass or brightly coloured containers they give a contemporary look, if placed in gold containers they give an elegant look, if placed in antique tins they give an old fashioned look or if placed in terracotta pots they give a cottage look.

Place a mirror on the dining room table and on it place a simple candle decoration. Alternatively put a glass bowl on the mirror containing floating candles.

Candles in front of mirrors also create a wonderful dancing light.

Tealights placed in glass containers provide an instant and inexpensive candle arrangement. Next time you shop buy a packet of 6 or 10 tealights and you will be surprised how effectively and artistically you can use them.

FOLLOWER CANDLE LAMP

These are one of the newer styles of candle holders and are most charming. They must be used with specially designed candles which have a ribbed end which sits securely in the candle holder. The candles have also been hardened to accommodate the weight of the lantern.

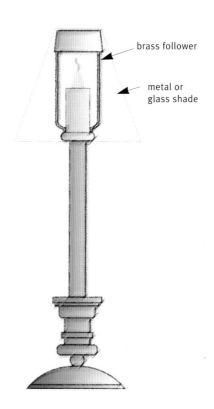

brass follower

metal or glass shade

Shades for these lanterns come in many different colours and patterns. I personally prefer the clear glass lanterns as I love to see the candle flicker.

As the candle burns down, the metal shade, which is held in place by the brass follower, lowers.

As with all candles, extinguish the flame before the follower reaches the holder.

I recently went to a restaurant where each table had a follower candle lamp on it. It was a real talking point. The candles had burnt for varying lengths of time and so were all different heights. I was amused to see two tables comparing their lights. Quite a good conversation piece.

A pair of follower candlesticks with clear glass lanterns.

CANDLES IN THE FIREPLACE

I have always been surprised by what some people put in the fireplaces in the off season. But why not fill the fireplace with candles?

The photograph on the front cover and on page 44 exudes a warm fuzzy feeling and is so simple to do. Any fireplace is suitable.

One of my friends, who is Swedish, has the most wonderful frame which sits in her fireplace. It holds candles of many sizes and when they are lit it is magic. You don't need to have anything quite as sophisticated as this. In one of our fireplaces we place lots of nuts and cones in the summer and have five tall fat candles sitting amongst them. This means that if the odd bit of soot or dust comes flying down the chimney it doesn't really matter as it is only the colour of the nuts and cones anyway and the candles can easily be wiped over with a cloth. It also means it is no distraction if the nuts and cones catch fire when the candles burn as it only means you need to find more nuts and cones!

Obviously there are lots of different ways to decorate the candle arrangements in the fireplace but whatever you do, it will look much nicer than having it bare and lighting the candles is just like having a fire but without as much heat. Gives a great atmosphere.

Suggested oils to use in the candles for fresh aroma are: Cedarwood, Orange and Bergamot / Juniper, Mandarin and Melissa / Lemon, Eucalyptus and Tangerine.

INDIVIDUAL CANDLE ARRANGEMENTS

I have always loved using individual candle arrangements at special dinners. Recently I discovered a source of unique very brightly coloured tiny cups and saucers which are candles. (See photograph on page 42.) One at each tablesetting is absolutely charming and a great conversation starter.

It is very easy to make your own cup and saucer candles—why not recycle your favourite but chipped Wedgewood cup and saucer? Treat it as a votive candle but make sure you heat the cup before pouring in the wax or the chip might turn into a crack very quickly. These candles can, of course, be refilled time and time again with wax.

Simple perfumed candles can be used as individual settings and because the candle is so close to everyone's nose they are a great conversation piece. When space in the centre of the table is precious then these individual candles can be a bonus.

BATHING BY CANDLELIGHT

One of life's best kept secrets—the candle-lit aromatherapy bath! You may like to have it by yourself or you may wish to share it with a friend.

One of the most beautiful things one can do to rejuvenate the body and spirit is to bathe by candlelight using essential oils. Baths have traditionally been used to improve health and beauty. The combination of essential oils and candlelight has a particularly calming and soothing effect, clearing the mind, relaxing the body and beautifying the skin. If you like, relaxing music can be played to enhance the atmosphere.

What you need

1   20 minutes of quality uninterrupted time.
2   2 really big, fat, fluffy soft towels.
3   A bathrobe.
4   A warm bathroom.
5   A bath full of warm water.
6   Aromatherapy candles.
7   Aromatherapy oils.

What to do

1   Place water and oils in bath.
2   Light candles—if these candles do not already have essential oils then add three or four drops to the melting wax of the candle. The essential oils are extremely volatile so be careful when putting them near the flame.
3   Turn out electric lights.
4   Ease yourself into the bath.
5   Place rolled towel behind your neck.
6   Breathe deeply.

What will happen?

Pure bliss—the flickering of the candles combined with their perfume makes this quite a mesmeric experience. You will wonder why you have left the bath unused for such a long time.

Suggested oil combinations for putting on candles and placing around the bath are:

To release stress	Bergamot, Sandalwood and Myrrh
To relax	Bergamot, Lavender and Cedarwood
To promote sleep	Bergamot, Orange and Lavender
Aphrodisiac	Ylang Ylang, Mandarin, Patchouli
Just to smell fresh	Lime, Grapefruit and Lemon
For men only	Cedarwood, Patchouli and Tangerine

CELEBRATION CANDLES

So often I have arrived at a function room with expensive lavish flowers to place amongst the pristine table arrangements and everything is just so perfect... except the smell! These rooms often smell of smoke and beer or yesterday's party.

So what do we do? Burn perfumed candles of course. This means we not only have the romantic light of the candle to create atmosphere but we also have the perfume created by these candles.

If you are making your own candles, add perfumed oils to the hot wax before you pour. If you already have unperfumed candles then add a few drops of oil to the melted wax on the candle.

It is very important when organising a function to make sure that your candles are not going to burn out before the function ends. A candle may say it will burn for 8 hours— however, with draughts and airconditioning, these candles will often burn for much less time. Burn a candle before the function under the same conditions to be sure. A rule of thumb is to add 50% burning time to the candle—that is, use a 9 hour candle for a 6 hour function.

NEVER buy cheap candles—generally, you get what you pay for so the cheaper the candle, the less time it burns.

I always insist on using my own candles when decorating for a function so I know they will outlast the party. It is not a good feel to have the candles fizzle out halfway through a wedding reception.

Always check with the venue to make sure candles can be used and, if so, it is a good idea to make sure they are smokeless as they can also set off smoke alarms. This can certainly take the intimacy away from the wedding speeches. If candles cannot be used, you will usually find you can use a tealight aromatherapy burner.

To create an air of celebration some suggested combinations of oils to put in candles are: Rosemary, Orange and Clove / Orange, May Chang and Palmarosa / Sage, Lemongrass and Bergamot.

USE OF GOLD AND SILVER

There is something very stylish about the colours gold and silver. An inexpensive plain coloured candle can be transformed by spraying with gold floral spray. You should be able to obtain this from reputable florist or craft shops. Don't use other cheaper sprays as the colour is too harsh and it is not as effective. With the floral spray waft it lightly over the candle and build up to required colour.

You can also apply it to inexpensive terracotta pots, candlesticks or even leaves or buds to add to the decoration. Lightly spray ivy or eucalyptus leaves and these will last for a very long time. The spray seems to preserve the leaves very well. Combine these with some of the stunning gold or silver organza ribbons available these days and you have a very professional arrangement.

An exotic collection of gold candles in the shape of cherubs, pears and balls.

My friend Carol, on New Year's Eve, had the most stunning simple candle decorations on her tables. In the centre of each table, on white cloths, she had three grey frosted glasses with a tealight candle in each. In a triangle around these she had simply sprayed some nuts, leaves and branches silver and placed them on the cloth. The effect was stunning, yet simple and achievable by any of us at very little cost.

CHRISTMAS

Christmas and candles definitely go together, whether it be decorating with them inside or outside. Carols by candlelight touches all our hearts.

This year, as we live in the southern hemisphere, my family had a Christmas party in the garden and we had red and green flare candles which were placed around the garden in safe spots as I did not want to set the garden alight. The citronella oil in these also kept the mosquitoes away.

Along my front path I had paper bags which I had painted red with acrylic paint and in them, set in sand, were my fat beeswax candles. I cut simple star shapes out of the bags and the light twinkled through as little stars.

At my front door I had my green candelabra which was planted in a pot of ivy holding five red candles. At the base of it I tied a tartan bow. Beside this was quite a large glass float bowl with red floating candles and a few small holly leaves. The same theme was repeated in my three bird baths which were placed in strategic positions in the garden.

On Christmas Eve night we lit our inside candles. They were all red and green this year.

I had a lovely star-shaped mould and so made several deep red candles of various heights. They were perfumed with the exotic essential oils of frankincense and myrhh and three sat at the centre of the servery on candle holders surrounded by fresh holly leaves. Others were placed in various positions around the house.

For my indoor candelabras I made red and green rolled beeswax candles using one sheet rolled on the longest side so they fit in the rather small holes. I did not perfume these as the wonderful honey smell is a perfect blend with the frankincense and myrhh of the other candles.

I made huge rolled beeswax candles of two heights by rolling some of them on the short side and some of them on the long side. Seven or eight sheets of beeswax were used to make each and they were so fat and stunning! These sat on the piano on simple glass candle-holders like a family. Because they were put out a month before Christmas I put bows around several of them which I removed before burning.
(See Rolled Beeswax Candles, page 46.)

In our dining room we always place our advent wreath in the centre of the table on the first day of December. On each of the four Sundays leading to Christmas we light a candle during dinner and then on Christmas Day we light the larger candle in the centre. This is a tradition held by our family for years and I hope my children carry it on as it is very special to me.

The Choir.

I have never put candles on my live Christmas tree as I feel it is far too unsafe, preferring to opt for fairy lights.

In our family room we have what we refer to as 'the Choir'— a group of white ceramic children either holding tiny red candles or with tea lights in their centres with the light coming through the star-shaped cut outs. (See photograph on page 58.) Lighting 'the Choir' is another ritual and is accompanied by a family member thumping out Christmas carols on the pianola.

Through the picture window in the family room is a weeping cherry and on one of the branches hangs an aluminium lantern with a red candle inside.

Something we did this year for the first time was to make our own scented beeswax ornaments to hang on the Christmas tree. To do this we collected several chocolate moulds in Christmas shapes. These were lightly oiled and then some pieces of wicking were cut in lengths of approximately 6–8 cms (2 1/2 – 3 inches) to form the loop to hang the ornaments from. We melted 500 grams (1 lb) beeswax in a double boiler and, when it was melted, I put in approximately 100 drops orange essential oil. The wax was then poured into the moulds with the loop of wicking placed at the top.

When set I turned the ornaments out of the mould and they were ready to hang on the tree. The rich colour and perfume of the beeswax combined with the perfume of the orange essential oil as well as the wonderful smell of our freshly cut Christmas tree (pinus radiata). It was addictive.

My friend Maggie takes a different approach to Christmas candles. Her house is very exotic and she has combinations of cream beeswax candles and fake greenery everywhere. There are tall black iron candleholders on the tables and underneath the big fat beeswax candles are wreaths of greenery (see Simple Candle Decoration, page 76) with gold organza bows of ribbon.

On the mantelpiece she has lots of greenery with very tall cream beeswax candles and across her long hearth are lots of small candles with wreaths of greenery at their base.

The enormous black iron candelabra which hangs under the skylight in the centre of the room has cream beeswax candles but underneath each candle is a bow of red satin ribbon.

EASTER

When we think of decorating for Easter we think of eggs and rabbits.

Rabbit moulds are easy to find and simple candles can be made by pouring paraffin and 10% stearic acid into these moulds as for a normal moulded candle. When they are turned out either drill a hole or use a hot skewer to create a hole for the primed wick to sit in. Pour hot wax to fill the hole after the wick is inserted.

We place our rabbit candle amongst some green jelly which has been mashed lightly with a fork—for no other reason than that is what we have always done.

Egg shells provide the most perfect moulds for candles. They are tiny and so it is not practical to make one at a time. Save your eggshells as you use the eggs, trying to keep about three quarters of the shell intact. Wash and dry them and put them back into the egg cartons.

An advent wreath for Christmas (see page 77).

You may wish to add yellow colouring which is the traditional Easter colour and only a little bit more effort.

Melt paraffin to 88°C (216°F) and add 10% stearic acid and perfumed oils but no colour. Fill the egg shells and leave to set for about twenty minutes. By this time the wax will have set around the shell just as egg white sits. Using a teaspoon remove the liquid wax from the centre of the candle and then pour in the wax mixture which has been reheated to 88°C (216°F) and had yellow colour added. This will form the egg yolk. Puncture and refill as normal.

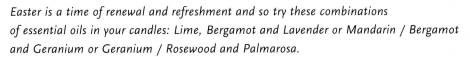

When the wax has set push a hot skewer into the wax and insert some fine primed wick. Fill the hole with hot wax.

You may wish to leave the eggs in their shells and perhaps place in an eggcup or alternatively they can have the egg shell broken away from them and with the bottoms smoothed they become free standing.

Easter is a time of renewal and refreshment and so try these combinations of essential oils in your candles: Lime, Bergamot and Lavender or Mandarin / Bergamot and Geranium or Geranium / Rosewood and Palmarosa.

For fresh flowers on my Easter table I like to make an arrangement of yellow and white daisies (Argyranthemum frutescens) and green box (Buxus sempervirons) leaves. I place these in a fairly formal way in a wet, green oasis ring base so I have a lovely arrangement of white, yellow and green. Then I fill the centre of the garland with moss and place several yellow dyed eggs in amongst it. On one side of the garland I place five white candles in candle holders amongst the flowers and put a drop of lime essential oil on the top of the candle. It looks beautiful and always brings favourable comment.

WEDDINGS

Candles are used at most wedding receptions these days. It is important when putting candle arrangements on tables to make sure they are very low or very high. There is nothing more annoying than having to compete with flowers and candles at eye level and so not being able to communicate across the table.

Recently I went to a wedding where the only table decorations were black iron candelabras standing about 1 metre high with three fat beeswax candles on them and a rich bow of gold wired ribbon tied at the neck. This decoration was simple but most effective as the room was mostly glassed and so there was a myriad of candles dancing around the room.

Most brides choose white or cream candles in keeping with the theme. These can be decorated with pressed flowers which repeat the flowers used in the wedding bouquets. For instance, if the bridal flowers are roses, lavender and orange blossom, then these can be pressed onto the candle (see Candles with Pressed Flowers, page 32) and the essential oils of rose, lavender and orange blossom (neroli) can be added

A simple candle decoration — flowers from my autumn garden in a terracotta pot with a rolled beeswax candle (see page 76).

to the candle as it is made or if the candles are bought then the oils can be added to the top of the candle before lighting.

Or simply add lush wired ribbons (perhaps the colour of the bridesmaids' dresses) to the candles or the candlesticks.

I find the addition of a candle to a very simple flower decoration makes a lot of impact. A little arrangement of flowers on a table can look a bit insignificant but the addition of the candle gives it a much better proportion. For this reason we have included the Simple Candle Decoration on page 76.

Simple bowls of floating candles, again with the theme flowers floating with the candles, are also a nice simple touch. Sometimes caterers and restaurants are a little precious about the amount of space the table decoration can take and so floating candles may not be ideal.

Table decorations of candles and fruit are fabulous. Place a nice large candle in the centre of a lovely bowl of fruit in season and you not only have a stunning arrangement but dessert as well. This can be as simple as an arrangement of red apples or in the middle of summer it could be an exotic arrangement of mangoes, peaches, nectarines, grapes and plumcots. Grapes are a particularly good shape to arrange.

If you really want to impress your friends and family you could wax the fruit. It gives a lovely Victorian look and makes for a great talking point. Simply dip the fruit in hot wax (approximately 88°C, 216°F) in a double boiler. Dip as many times as you wish, depending on the effect you want. The wax will not preserve the fruit but the wax can be peeled off and the fruit eaten.

If there is only one oil which you use in your candles for a wedding then it should be rose oil. Rose is a symbol of love and purity and petals are strewn at weddings to ensure a happy marriage.

VALENTINE'S DAY

For Valentine's Day we can obviously make candles to float in the shape of hearts or perhaps stencil red hearts on to a regular candle. However this is a time when it would be nice to concentrate on the essential oils to put in the candle.

Use combinations of the exotic essential oils: Ylang Ylang, Clary Sage, Rose, Neroli, Jasmine, Sandalwood.

Or you could use: Rose and Ylang Ylang with Bergamot / Ylang Ylang and Jasmine with Patchouli / Rose and Patchouli with Orange.

Remember, Ylang Ylang is the aphrodisiac oil and rose is the oil of love.

A candlelit dinner with the perfume of the essential oils, good food and good company makes for a very special occasion.

A mystical photograph of a 5-pronged candelabra in a pot planted with ivy and lobelia on a table in my garden.

CANDLES IN THE GARDEN

One of the most wonderful accessories for making outside candle arrangements is a green powder-coated candlestick which holds either three or five candles. This can be obtained from leading nurseries. If you are unable to purchase these candlesticks or would rather make your own then this can be done quite easily.

Take a garden pot which suits the proportion of the candlestick. Place the feet of the candleholder in the bottom of the pot and 3/4 fill the pot with a high quality potting mix. Place a plant of a small leafed climber such as Ivy (Hedera helix), Chinese Star Jasmine (Trachelospernum) or Maidenhair Creeper (Muehlenbeckia complexa) as close to the stem as possible and fill the pot with more potting mix, adding a good fertilizer. As the plant grows train it to wind around the frame, cutting off any stems which you do not need.

For the photograph opposite, I have placed a 3 pronged candlestick in a lovely oval shaped terracotta pot. In the pot I have planted a small leafed ivy and then at the bottom of the pot I have planted Alyssum (Lobularia maritima) which has a rosy pink flower. I have then placed green candles in the candlestick and against the pink wall on my verandah it looks very elegant.

The five pronged candlestick on page 64 also has a small leafed ivy winding around its trunk. The pot is planted with lobelia which spills all over the edge making a living flower arrangement. We always keep pots like this in our nursery and they are often used to decorate churches and wedding receptions.

In the photograph on the back cover I have attached 3 cream beeswax candles to this lovely harp frame which is planted with Maidenhair creeper. I first designed this frame to decorate a stage for a chamber music concert. I had ten of these in terracotta pots on pedestals in a straight line across the back of the stage and with the candles alight it provided a very romantic background to this lovely concert. We now make them in our nursery all the time.

Sometimes you may not have enough time to prepare this growing candlestick but never fear—the frames by themselves are most attractive and so if the plant hasn't grown very much you can attach a bow of ribbon to the frame to make it more festive. You can also fake greenery by cutting it from another plant placing it in a phial of water and burying it at the stem of the plant. This can make an instant mature plant.

These stunning arrangements can be brought inside for special occasions or left permanently on an outside table or perhaps at the entrance to your house.

We also have a wonderful A-frame shape which, when covered with a small leaf climber, takes on a two- dimensional Christmas tree shape. When a candle is placed at the base and a red bow of ribbon added it is a perfect living Christmas tree.

My 3-pronged powder-coated candlestick in an oval terracotta pot planted with ivy and lobelia.

For many years I have placed candles to identify the entrance to my front door. These have been fat candles placed in a bed of sand in a big brown paper bag which has a gusset in the bottom. This means there is plenty of room between the flame and the bag. The bag protects the flame from the wind and the light displayed is magic.

In our nursery over the years we have spent much time creating outside candle arrangements.

A garden bowl planted with a simple green plant looks charming with a candle sitting in the middle. Choose a candle with the right proportions for the pot. Just place it amongst your other potted plants outside and it will create a real focus once the sun goes down. We once decorated the entrance to a house with grey 'apostle' pots, planted with 'baby's tears' (Helix soleirolii), in a row down a very formal front path and in each one was a fat beeswax candle. It was simple and stunning and most appropriate for the formal occasion.

The pot of 'baby's tears' (opposite) has three blue candles tucked into the foliage. These candles are put in candle holders (see page 73) which are pushed into the soil. This means they will not fall over. This is a simple instant garden arrangement and can be brought inside for special occasions or kept outside. Similarly the pot of baby's tears (below) just has one fat candle placed in the centre of the foliage. How simple is that!

You can put a candle in almost any planted garden pot. It might mean having to be a bit resourceful and perhaps placing a candlestick amongst the flowers and foliage. The candle should always be high to prevent a fire.

A pot of baby's tears with a single candle placed in it.

A pot of baby's tears with three blue taper candles.

Candles in terracotta pots are a charming addition to any garden. The pots are inexpensive to buy and can be placed in a row on a table, up a garden path or simply amongst other garden pots. The light exuded is lovely and of course they can be refilled with wax over and over again. Ready made or tea light candles can be placed in these pots if you do not have time to make them.

On one of my outside tables I have two candelabras made with terracotta pots. The bottom pot is 13 1/2 cms (5 1/2 inches) in diameter and in it I have placed some sand about 3/4 of the way up the centre of the pot and all around the sides. In this I have placed a 12 cm (5 inch) pot and packed sand around so it sits securely. I have then placed five more 12 cm (5 inch) pots inside each other, securing with sand if necessary. Then I have placed a tall citronella candle packed in sand in the top pot so it stands straight. In between these two candelabras I have a terracotta bowl of blooming plants. Looks great!

Citronella (Cymbopogon nardus) is a tall, aromatic, perennial grass which is native to Sri Lanka. An essential oil is derived from it by steam distillation and we traditionally use it as an insect repellant.

Citronella oil is most effective if added to the candle as it is made. However, it is always possible to add a couple of drops to any candle and this will act as an effective insect repellent when you are outside.

Candle flares are a wonderful source of garden lighting plus they are normally perfumed with citronella oil for keeping the bugs at bay. They are great for identifying paths or entranceways and usually have nice long stems for pushing into the ground. Because the flames from them are quite high be very careful where you place them.

They come in happy bright primary colours and so different colours can be picked out for different themes, e.g. yellow for Easter or red and green for Christmas. Last Christmas in the nursery we made bunches of red and green candles and tied them together with green and red raffia. Great gifts for garden or party people. In the photograph here I have placed brightly coloured flares in pots of very brightly coloured flowers and the reflections at night are amazing. The room on the other side of the window has bright jewel colours in the accessories and so the inside/outside combination is stunning. At Christmas I will change the flowers in the pots to red and have red and green flares placed amongst them.

Floating candles placed in birdbaths or float bowls in the garden can be charming. Floating candles can be bought in many shapes and colours. The floating candles on page 34 are taken in one of our ponds and are the shape of a large sunflower.

Candle lamps are also very suitable outside. We have a pair which we have been using on an outside table for years and because the flame is protected by the clear glass container there is no chance of it blowing out.

Brightly coloured flare candles tone with the pots
of brightly coloured flowers in my courtyard.

USING CANDLES IN FLOWER ARRANGEMENTS

Before showing you how to make some exquisite but simple flower arrangements with candles there is one small florist supply which you need to know about.

After all the years I have taught flower arranging I am still amazed that so few people know about this. It is a plastic candle holder which is very cheap to buy and it accommodates a normal candle. Designed to fit into the florist foam, whether it be wet or dry, the holder stabilises the candle and stops it moving about. It also adds about 3–4 cms (1 1/2–2 inches) to the height of the candle and it is so simply designed that you cannot even see it in the arrangement. They are also wonderful from a commercial point of view as arrangements can be transported without any fear of the candles falling and making holes in the oasis. We use them in our shop all the time.

If the size of the candle is such that it does not fit into this candleholder then the most secure way to place the candle is as follows:

Take 4 pieces of size 18 wire which are approximately 10 cms (4 inches) long. Tape the wires to the candle using florist tape or electrical tape with 1/2 the wire below the candle and 1/2 the wire taped to the candle. This will give the candle legs which will sit in the oasis safely and keep the candle sitting high.

Take note that there are different laws in different states about the sale of candles and flowers together.

TAKE GREAT CARE WHEN LIGHTING CANDLES IN FLOWER ARRANGEMENTS TO MAKE SURE THAT THERE IS NO RISK OF FIRE.

An arrangement with Australian Native Flowers and Candles.

A DECORATED CANDLESTICK

Often you have a plain candlestick which just needs a bit of smartening up. By using this method you can make the candlestick as simple or as elaborate as you wish. You could just use pieces of fake greenery with red bows for a Christmas look or a wreath of more elaborate flowers may be used for a wedding table. All you are doing is making a wreath of flowers to attach to the candlestick.

Equipment

Cutters

Glue gun

Ingredients

Green florist wire, sizes 20 and 24

Green parafilm

Flowers, nuts and berries

This arrangement is usually more practical using fake or dried instead of fresh flowers as it is too hard to keep the fresh flowers alive, especially when affected by the heat of the candle. However, if you do use fresh flowers you can extend their life by spraying frequently with water.

HOW TO MAKE THE ARRANGEMENT

1   Measure the size 20 wire to the length of the wreath required to sit around the candlestick. Cut, allowing 2.5 cms (1 inch) overlap at each end.

2   Make small bunches of flowers binding them with fine size 24 wire.

3   Tie each bunch along the wreath wire with fine florist wire, overlapping each one so you don't see any of the wires.

4.   Bend the decorated wire into the wreath shape and attach to candlestick by forming a 'U' shape at each end of the wire with the overlap and attaching inside each other. The flowers of the first bunch should overlap the flowers of the last bunch.

5   Use a glue gun to attach any extra flowers needed to fill in gaps, or perhaps to add some bows. Sometimes a dab of glue may be needed to secure the wreath to the candlestick.

A decorated candlestick with fake fruit and cones.

A SIMPLE CANDLE DECORATION

This simple candle decoration is very useful for many occasions. An arrangement with a few flowers can look lost in the middle of a table but as soon as you add a candle with its flickering light it can be transformed into a real showpiece.

You can use any variation of flowers in these arrangements whether they are fresh or dry. You could also use only greenery and add a few bows or in winter when there is a scarcity of flowers just use greenery with Sacred Bamboo (Nandina domestica) berries or perhaps rose hips. It is often very effective to use whatever flowers, foliage or berries are in season.

On the other hand if the occasion calls for extravagance this arrangement can be made on a much larger scale using more or bigger candles.

The arrangement on page 73 uses flowers from the garden in autumn. The container is a terracotta pot which complements the arrangement.

Equipment

Cutters

Ingredients

Terracotta pot

Frog (a four pronged plastic holder)

Florist surestick

Floral foam

Candleholder

Candle

Flowers, foliage, berries

HOW TO MAKE THE ARRANGEMENT

1   Secure frog to centre bottom of container with surestick.

2   Cut florist foam so it sits at least 2.5 cm (1 inch) above the side of the container. Place oasis on frog.

3   Place candleholder in centre of florist foam and position candle.

4   Place greenery in a symmetrical way covering the florist foam spreading long trails on elongated arrangements.

5   Build up the design with flowers and berries alternating colour, shape and texture. (If using fresh flowers make sure you soak the oasis first).

AN ADVENT WREATH

'Advent' means arrival or coming and in a Christian sense it is the season including the four Sundays immediately preceding the festival of the Nativity. Many countries celebrate this event with an advent wreath—burning a candle on each of the four Sundays and quite often a fifth candle is placed in the centre of the wreath to burn on Christmas Day. The candles for the four Sundays are usually red and the Christmas Day candle is white. Make sure you have long burning candles and why not perfume them with some exotic Christmas oils to set the atmosphere (e.g. frankincense and myrhh).

Equipment

Cutters

Ingredients

Fake pine

Dark green
dried leaves

Dried white
sago flowers

12 dried red
helichrysum flowers

12 gold pinecones

12 large red balls

8 gold gumnuts

Florist foam wreath

Spanish moss

Small pins (fine wires
cut to 'U' shapes)

4 candle holders

4 candles

4 m (4 yards) ribbon

HOW TO MAKE THE ARRANGEMENT

1. Place candleholders equidistant from each other in florist foam wreath and place candles in position.

2. Cover the oasis with Spanish moss using small pins.

3. Place pine in oasis creating a loose green cover over the top and sides.

4. Fill in gaps with small pieces of green gum and white sago flowers.

5. Make four simple bows each from 1 metre (1 yard) of ribbon and attach a wire to them.

6. Place bows midway between candles, across the top of the wreath.

7. Finally add helichrysum flowers, nuts, red balls, and cones evenly dispersed over the wreath.

This is a description of the wreath we have photographed on page 60. This is just one method—the wreath can just as easily be made with a mixture of fresh green foliages, especially conifer as it lasts very well, and any mixture of red flowers, nuts and berries. With fresh flowers make sure the florist foam has been soaked before placing the flowers.

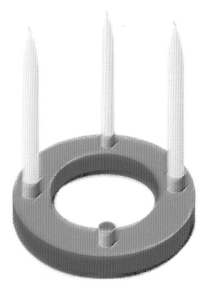

AN ARRANGEMENT WITH AUSTRALIAN NATIVE fLOWERS AND CANDLES

This is a natural looking flower arrangement which sits in a complementary wooden box and is filled with gorgeous glycerine-dried eucalyptus leaves and blossoms. It is shown on page 72.

Equipment

Cutters

Ingredients

1 1/2 blocks grey florist foam

2 frogs

surestick

Spanish moss

2 beeswax candles

No 18 and No 22 florists wire

pot tape

eucalyptus foliage, blue and red

eucalyptus blossom

eucalyptus nuts (approximately 20)

sago flowers

grey wooden box approximately 28 cms x 15 cms (11 inches x 6 inches)

HOW TO MAKE THE ARRANGEMENT

1   Fill box with grey florist foam to 2 cm (1 inch) above edge. Tape 4 x 10 cm (4 inches) pieces of No 18 wire like feet, to base of candles, and insert evenly spaced into oasis.

2   Cover oasis with Spanish moss, attached with small wire pins made from size 22 florist wire.

3   Take 2 x 25 cm (10 inches) pieces eucalyptus foliage (curved, if possible) and place at centre of each end of box horizontally, curving down. Place 1 x 20 cm (8 inches) piece of curved eucalyptus front and back of box—horizontally. Two x 25 cm (10 inches) pieces should be inserted at either end of box, at 45˚ angle—still curving down. Next, corner pieces, then fill in gaps with more eucalyptus foliage.

4   Eucalyptus blossom should be placed between eucalyptus foliage, evenly dispersed—with some pieces curving down over sides of box.

5   Sago flowers, too, should be placed in any remaining gaps, a little deeper in the arrangement than the foliage and the blossom.

6   Finally, eucalyptus nuts should be wired (No 22 wires) and placed at random throughout the arrangement.

CARE Of CANDLES

1 To lengthen the burning time of a candle, store in the freezer until needed.

2 To avoid candles becoming distorted, always store in a cool place.

3 Candles should always be left for 24 hours after making to cure them.

4 If possible, burn candles for 4 hours at a time to keep them in good condition.

5 Candles mark very easily from handling but can be buffed with a cloth (an old piece of silk is perfect) and rubbed with a small amount of almond oil.

6 Trim candle wicks to approximately 2 cms (3/4 inch) before relighting and this will stop excessive smoking.

7 Keep candles out of draughts or they will burn much quicker and the melting wax may become messy.

8 Always place candles perfectly upright or they will drip.

9 To blow out a candle without splattering, place your index finger between you and the flame and blow.

10 Store wax for candlemaking in a dry cool place away from dust.

PRECAUTIONS

1 Never leave burning candles unattended.

2 Always melt wax in a double boiler.

3 When making candles never leave wax unattended on a flame.

4 If wax ignites it must be extinguished by smothering with a towel or a lid. It is a good idea to keep a towel close by just in case. Never throw water on wax.

5 Never pour wax down a drain.

6 If hot wax is spilled on to skin, don't wipe it off but run cold water over it until it solidifies and then scrape it off.

7 If wax is spilled on tablecloths or clothing allow it to set and then scrape it off. It is a good idea to then have the garment or cloth professionally cleaned if it is special. Placing paper or blotting paper either side and ironing it will remove the wax but will set the wax dye if it has colour in it.

8 When using ribbons and flowers (particularly dried flowers) with burning candles be very careful not to let the burning wick come into contact with them as they can be quite flammable.

9 Always secure candle in a non-flammable heat-resistant receptacle.

THE MOST COMMON PROBLEMS WITH CANDLES

1   Frost marks on candle

The wax was poured too cold. Remake candle.

2   Smoking candle

The wick is too thick and the candle does not have enough wax to burn. Also the wick may be too long.

3   Wax drips down side of candle

Candle placed in a draught or candle wick is too small.

4   Flame extinguished by molten wax

Candle wick is too small or the wick sits too loosely in the candle.

5   The candle has a mottled surface

The wax was cooled too slowly.

6   The candle spits while burning

Water in the candle.

7   Sides of candle cave in

Air in centre of candle so candle not probed enough around wick.

8   Small bubbles around the candle

The water level in the water bath was not deep enough.

9   Candle will not burn

The wick has not been primed—sometimes by holding the candle upside down it will light.

10 Candle is difficult to remove from mould

Usually this is because there is not enough stearic acid in the wax mix—place in refrigerator for an hour and it should unmould easily. If not, wipe mould with a hot wet cloth until it is removed.

RESTORING CANDLES

If you have candles that are looking a bit tired or you wish to change the colours, then try dipping them. This disguises many defects and flaws on the surface, and produces a perfect looking new candle. It is also a wonderful way of changing the colour of the candle.

Prepare your wax (90% paraffin wax and 10% stearic acid and add colour and essential oils) and heat to 82°C (180°F) and using tweezers or pliers, dip the candle in the wax for about 3 seconds and withdraw quickly. If you wish to have a shiny finish then dip into cold water immediately. For a dull finish don't dip but cool slowly.

Make sure the wax is the right temperature. If it is too cool then it will not fix properly. If it is too hot it will not colour properly. Redip, if necessary, until you reach the required colour. You could layer the colours—dip the whole candle in one colour and then redip half the candle in another colour. You could do as many layers as you wish. Candles which are dipped give a much denser colour than solid coloured candles. They also fade less.

sources

Hands at Work
28 Viking Court
Cheltenham VIC 3122

Poyco Candle Co Pty Ltd
164–168 Burwood Road
Hawthorn VIC 3122

W R Designs
PO Box 7
Brighton SA 5048

Candlecraft
42–44 Kingston Road
Camperdown NSW 2050

Ablaze Wholesalers
44–52 Taplin Street
North Fitzroy VIC 3068

Willie Winkle Candles
97 Fairey Road
South Windsor NSW 2756

Redpath Beekeeping Supplies
193 Como Parade East
Parkdale VIC 3195

Pialligo Plant Farm
12 Beltana Road
Pialligo ACT 2609

Rhondda Cleary

Since 1980, Rhondda Cleary has been the creative force behind the Pialligo Plant Farm, a plant nursery, flower decorating centre and botanical school on the outskirts of Australia's national capital, Canberra.

Rhondda's Farm is a happening place where she organises all types of flower-related activities, from growing and drying and arranging, to workshops on diverse topics such as flower arranging, aromatherapy, papermaking, lavender farming and, of course, candlemaking.

Rhondda's interest in candlemaking began when she started combining candles with plant material to create festive decorations for special social events, both in homes, and on a larger scale. Her work has been used to enhance vast spaces such as the Great Hall in Australia's Parliament House, and the foyer of Australia's National Gallery.

In all her creations Rhondda aims to appeal to the sense of smell as well as to that of sight and to achieve the results she wanted she had to make her own candles. Now she shares her work in this book.